POLISH WYCINANKI DESIGNS

Frances Drwal

Stemmer
House
Publishers

Gilsum, NH 03448

To John, Terry and Ann
without whom this book would not have been

INTRODUCTION

As long as there have been people on earth, they have found a way to express themselves in some form of art. When this is done by ordinary people, it is called folk art. Folk artists use whatever materials they have at hand, their tools are their everyday utensils, and their art shows what they feel and see around them. They show their activities, what surrounds them, whatever pleases them. They need follow no particular rules except their own and use their art functionally or decoratively. Most folk artists are country folk, and their art is enjoyed only by them and those close to them. It could be lost to the rest of the world, were it not for people who discover, or rather, uncover, it and make it known to others. Thus it was with the Polish folk art of wycinanki (vih-chee-náhn-kee). The word wycinanki comes from the Polish verb "wycinác" which means to cut; wycinanki meaning things that are cut, or papercuts.

Papercuts such as the Polish wycinanki, so varied and colorful and used decoratively, are to be found nowhere else but in Poland. How it happened that wycinanki appeared and developed in this form solely in Poland no one can truly say. We can, however, say that wycinanki began in some rural areas of Poland. Here people were close to nature, depended mainly on themselves for all aspects of thier existence. Of necessity, they used their everyday utensils in any way they found them to be useful. It is thus that sheep shears came to be the tool responsible for the folk art of wycinanki. It is not known when this came about. It has been stated, and probably erroneously, that wycinanki had their beginning in Poland in the late 19th century, probably because this is the time colored paper appeared on the scene. However, Anna Kordecki, a well known papercutter from the Kurpie region of Poland, tells that wycinanki were made there from paper which was colored by hand by papercutters. White wycinanki also exist. While it is true that wycinanki were uncovered in the later 19th century, they were probably being made long before that time. Nevertheless, wycinanki as an art form were late in being discovered and given recognition. They became popular in Polish folk ornamentation in the 19th century and flourished in the first quarter of the 20th century, as evidenced by the collections of Gerson, a lover of Polish folk arts.

From the motifs in the collections of Gerson of the oldest wycinanki, it would point to the area around Warsaw as the birthplace of this folk art. In these, we find the most simple original forms of the tree, one of the fundamental motifs, which is then found in the two main regional modifications of wycinanki — those of Kurpie and Lowicz. The white wycinanki also persisted in the Warsaw area. However unclear are the beginnings of wycinanki in Poland, let us look at wycinanki themselves. In their classic form, they are abstract ornaments put together rhythmically and, in the main, symmetrically to several axes. This is done by means of a most simple technique : shears, most of the large shears used for clipping sheep are used to cut through paper which has been folded, in some wycinanki once, and in some, over and over. On unfolding, you behold a characteristic design, not so much through its make-up as through specifically simple cuts of scissors which results in the ornamental open work. The folds and cuts are in short, usually diagonal lines, less often slightly curved, creating the specific wycinanki motifs such as arrows, little comb teeth, diamonds, lenticular leaves or strands of thickly concentrated strokes. All this is cut without any previous preparation, without any stiffness, and enlivened with tiny deviations from the motif. Wycinanki of this type may be in the shape of a wheel, stars, squares or diamonds and sometimes long strands. Aside from these, there are vertical trees, human forms, joined mostly horizontally, rhythmical rows, schematically cut roosters and birds. With these themes, the main effect depends on the symmetrical silhouettes adorned by tinier open cuts. In some regions such simple wycinanki are not common. The more complicated wycinanki are composed of various layers of brightly colored paper one atop the other in ribbons or strands. The themes are flowers, scenes with people, mainly weddings and other feasts. Wycinanki in Poland are used exclusively as decorations. In many parts of Poland, interiors of cottages were decorated with wycinanki — these were glued either onto the walls or onto the ceiling or onto the ceiling beams. It should be emphasized that decorating homes with wycinanki was not tied in with any particular customs or rites, although this was done prior to Easter. Farmsteads were usually decorated in this manner once a year, just after the customary pre-Easter whitewashing of the walls; the yearly Easter whitewashing of the outside of the cottages remained until recently a part of the village ritual.

Undoubtedly, it is only by chance — because they were in the surroundings of the folk artists — that roosters, chickens, and birds appear in wycinanki. They were introduced just as was the peacock, silhouetted trees, doll figures and flowers, in consideration of thier attractive forms. Polish wycinanki were strictly made as decorations — an exception to the general rule of folk art that the artistic side of it is always only the form or supplement of the useful side.

Wycinanki can be divided into two main groups: the first group consists of one-color wycinanki which are made of one piece of paper folded once or several times, in which one pattern is cut out. The second group comprises multi-colored wycinanki or several layers pasted one on the other, the designs being flowers, birds, human figures or genre scenes.

At present, the making of wycinanki is popular in several regions of Poland, the two main areas being Kurpie and Lowicz. The most typical of the Kurpie paper wycinanki is a one-color symmetric papercut, which is called a leluja (leh-loo-yah). These may be open at the top or closed to resemble a monstrance. The forest or woodland cuts, requiring a slight variation in the folding, are very attractive. Also popular are wycinanki with a symmetric pattern in a circle, one-color thematic picture wycinanki, and multi-colored ones in the shape of roosters. The Lowicz wycinanki are usually multi-colored ones of various shapes and forms: round (the gwiazdy or stars), in the form of a ribbon with a circle (kodry), ribbons or stripes, multi-thematic picture wycinanki and wycinanki pasted onto egg shells. Designs for all these are included in this book. Today it is rare for wycinanki to serve their original purpose, for few people in the Polish countryside decorate their cottages in this manner. But the village women and girls still cut out wycinanki —for people from the city.

It is hoped that the information and designs in this book will encourage a new wave of papercutting and that wycinanki will adorn many an American home.

Frances Drwal

Designs 1 through 10 are of the leluja type of wycinanki. One fold is made in the paper, and the result, after cutting, is a symmetric papercut. Designs 1 and 2 are open at the top, while the remainder resemble a monstrance. Each set of two wycinanki facing each other contain a variety of cuts as described in the introduction.

Designs 11 through 14 are the forest or woodland wycinanki. To make these, a lengthwise fold is made in the middle of a rectangular sheet of paper. It is then folded once more in half, lengthwise. The cuts are made on both edges of the folded paper.

Designs 15 through 20 are of the "gwiazdy" or star type of wycinanki. A square piece of paper is folded diagonally to form a triangle; this is folded in half again and once again, if the thickness of the paper permits. The folded paper will have the shape of a piece of pie. Cuts are then made on the folded sides of the paper.

Designs 24 and 25 and 26 and 27 are thematic wycinanki, depicting scenes from village life. Each piece is cut separately and then layered to complete the picture.

Designs 35 through 40 are layered birds and roosters of the Lowicz type. While designs 41 through 44 are also layered wycinanki, these are flowers and trees.

Design 32 is of the "kodry" type, the circle being cut first and layered, the two ribbons cut together and then also layered.

Designs 33 and 34 are a variety of the ribbon wycinanki.

Designs 45 and 46 are the medallion wycinanki, which are a combination of the single fold and layered papercuts.

Design 39 is a symmetric pattern in a circle. The paper for this is folded like that for the star designs, with sections left uncut, leaving these parts for layering with other designs.

Design 47 is a layered Lowicz flower.

Designed by Barbara Holdridge
Composed by Brown Composition, Inc.,
Baltimore, Maryland
Cover printed by Strine Printing Co.,
York, Pennsylvania
Text printed on 75-pound Williamsburg Offset
and bound by Victor Graphics, Inc.,
Baltimore, Maryland